A Poem for All Seasons

PALMETTO
PUBLISHING
Charleston, SC
www.PalmettoPublishing.com

Copyright © 2024 by Abigail Rose Fucci

All rights reserved

No portion of this book may be reproduced, stored in a retrieval system, or transmitted in any form by any means–electronic, mechanical, photocopy, recording, or other–except for brief quotations in printed reviews, without prior permission of the author.

Paperback ISBN: 9798822960503

A Poem for All Seasons

ABIGAIL ROSE FUCCI

Dedicated to my parents,
Timothy Heisler, my junior year English teacher,
and other young aspiring poets.

Table of Contents

Spiritual and Inspirational Poems 1

Seasonal Poems 55

New Life Poems 69

Love Poems 81

Grief Poems 109

School Poems 141

Miscellaneous Poems 159

Short Verses 193

About the Author 198

Spiritual and Inspirational Poems

A Prayer of Inspiration

You are a daughter of God; you have expectations. Only give yourself to one man on your wedding day. Keep your allure hidden; it is powerful and should be used wisely. Dress modestly. Be kind. Be respectful. Love everyone. Be optimistic.

You have the power of PIE.

You are strong, bold, courageous.

Focus on the present moment. This is important.

Focus on Jesus. He is all things good.

Do not focus too much on the future. That is not the goal. It can be a distraction.

Make friends. Live in the present. Find friends who understand you and who will support you.

Pray, pray, pray!!!

Prayer of Praise

My precious Savior
In the monstrance,
Beautiful to behold
And radiant as the sun,
So tender and loving,
Yet also rendering justice.

So many rays of mercy and graces
Shine forth from the monstrance
Piercing my heart and others,
Going into the depths of my soul.
A transformation is working,
However imperceptible it may be.

May I bring forth Your love,
Your mercy, Your compassion
To all I encounter,
To all who may need it.
Blessed be my Lord and Savior
Forever and ever. Amen.

Beautiful Child (song)

Blessed are you my dear children! You have trusted in me, you have loved me. Remember that I love you, that I care for you! You are my sheep!

My beautiful child, stay true to me and forget me not. Lord, You are the love of my life, you are my strength!

Be kind to each other and hate your brother not. Say to him "I love you." Expect nothing in return.

Do not worry my little one! My mother, Mary, has you in her arms. Do not trouble yourself further, for your life is in my hands.

My Son died for your life, He died so you might live! Remember the poor, the outcast, the forgotten. Have a caring heart for all you see.

I know your suffering! I know your pain! Fall into my arms! I thirst for you! My child, you are beautiful, you are loved! You are the apple of my eye!

The plans I have for you are great to behold! You are the splendor of my life, my comfort, and my joy! Take care in all you do. Remember, I am always here for you.

Chains of Life

Life's obstacles can be so frustrating,
They seem never-ending, year-round.
It seems we're being dragged down
And torn to pieces in our daily lives.

Sometimes life feels like a pain,
We wonder why evil is allowed to exist.
So many atrocities befall us,
It can seem like God had forgotten us.

We may react badly to such evil,
We may get mad at God for its presence.
We may lose our faith in God,
And give up the hope that things will improve.

In this earthly life,
We form the chains of our life.
Our actions, words, everything in life
Forges the chain we carry to the next life.

Are we forming a chain
That will strangle us?
Are we forming chains
That might suffocate us?

Chains aren't really good things.
They are meant to drag us down.
We must take care to avoid evil
And break these life's chains.

God allows all to happen
For reasons unknown to us.
Rest assured my good friends,
The reasons He has are good!

Life isn't meant to be easy.
The sure path to Heaven
Isn't a leisurely, luxurious lifestyle.
It isn't quite that simple.

The path to Heaven is narrow.
It's windy and filled with obstacles.
We will face daily challenges,
And we will fall many times.
God won't leave us alone though.
He wants us in Heaven with Him.
He is always by our side,
Especially when life seems impossible.

God doesn't want us
To form heavy chains in life.
However, if such chains are formed,
God will help us break them.

If we follow Jesus and our faith,
Stay true to our authentic selves,
We can live in Christ's love,
And avoid these chains of life.

Floundering at Sea

Sometimes in my life
I feel like a fish
Floundering in the sea,
Lost in total darkness.

I swim around and around,
Trying to find the light.
I bump into things often
And stray off the right path.

The waters get colder and colder,
Near to a freezing point.
I have lost my way,
And wonder how to get back.

I push on and on
Until I ache all over.
I feel numb and tired,
And can't continue on.

Lo and behold though
I see a sliver of light.
I swim towards it,
Aiming to enter that light.

But I can't seem to get there.
I'm not strong enough.
My body is run down,
Feeling lifeless and scared.

I give one last shot,
I have some energy left.
I swim to the surface,
And fly up out of the water.

For a brief second, I can see!
I see the light and the sun,
The warm air is embracing,
My heart soars again.

I land back in the waters,
Wishing to be in the light.
Then suddenly I see
The light coming to me.

The Son reaches out His hands,
And pulls me out of the darkness.
The Holy Spirit warms me up,
And I feel on fire for God.

He takes me to His bosom
And holds me tight.
He then lets me go,
But with renewed vigor and strength.

I no longer swim in darkness.
I am not floundering at sea.
I have seen the Son, the light,
That dispels all darkness.

I now walk in the light of Christ,
With a leap in my walk.
My heart is light and cheery,
Powered by the Son of God.

Good Friday

Step by step
And inch by inch
Our Savior did trod
On His way to Calvary.

The crowd continued chanting
For Him to be crucified.
Only a select few were
Mourning and weeping for him.

He was spat upon,
Bruised, cursed, mocked, and beaten.
Yet not a cry sounded
Or escaped from His lips.

He bore it all quietly,
And patiently trodded on.
The soldiers' constant beatings
Caused Him to fall several times.

Mama Mary followed in agony
Her Son's road to Calvary.
A sword would pierce her heart,
A pain none of us will know.

His beloved disciple
And the faithful women of Jerusalem
Followed in His footsteps,
With tears flowing like a fountain.

His garments were stripped off
So roughly that the skin came too.
The soldiers cast lots
To fulfill the prophesies.

He was nailed to a tree
For our sins and transgressions.
God's wrath was upon Him,
For He felt abandoned.

He breathed His last
Three hours past noon.
His spirit was released
To carry out its bidding.
While those on earth wept,
Those in the netherworld
Were joyful to the core,
Having waited for years for this to come.

Heaven's gates were opened—
Cries of joy at last!
It had to be done this way,
Just as the Father desired.

Let us remember this moment,
That Christ bore all for us.
Let us try to help lighten
The load He carried for us.

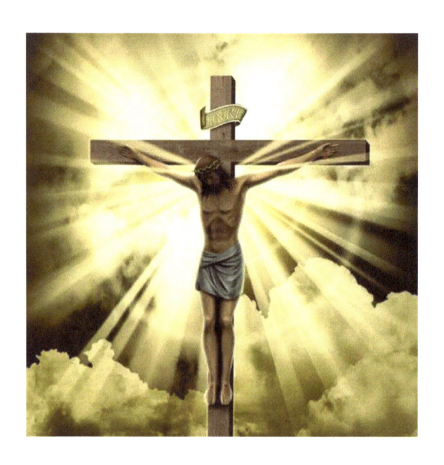

Jesus, It's Been Too Long

It's been a while
Since I've been here.
It's been too long
Without seeing you.

I can't even believe
That it's been so long,
Or that I've forgotten you,
Pushed you out of my life.

Oh, dear Jesus,
I'm so sorry.
I've been a fool,
Stubborn, pigheaded, and stupid.

I feel so guilty
That I've been busy,
That I put you second
When you should be first.

My life has been nuts,
So hectic and confusing.
Things have gone awry,
Even upside-down.

I realize I gotta do something,
I need to make you a priority.
You should always be first,
I need to keep you at the center.

Everything comes second
And you come first.
My priorities need fixing,
And they will be fixed.

Please Holy Spirit,
Help me with this.
Help me to put God first,
To put Him at the center of everything.

I know I need adoration,
To do it once a week at least.
And with that things will improve,
And all will fall into place.
Thank you, Lord, for everything,
For my life, job, and school.
For my friends, family, and boyfriend,
And most of all for Jesus, my Savior.

Life will get better,
I just know it will.
In time I now see
That the pieces will fall into place.

Jesus

I come to the chapel
In the eve of day-
When the sun sets
And dusk becomes one.

I go to a pew-
And kneel and sit.
Just stare at Jesus
In the monstrance-behold!

The monstrance so lovely,
And shining like the sun
Ever so brightly
Puts forth its rays.

The host inside
Is my beautiful Savior.
His Body and Blood-
And Soul and Divinity!

My King of kings,
Prince of princes,
Richest of the rich,
Poorest of the poor.

The moment together-
I cherish so much.
All I can say is-
"I love you, Jesus, my Savior!"

Letting Go (song)

This week has been unreal—
Like I'm livin' in a dream.
I wanna say to myself
Wake up! And just let go!

I wanna let go-o-o,
I wanna let go-o-o,
I wanna wake up,
And see what's coming in.

So, let's wake up! Let's let go of our past,
Our mistakes and our missed chances,
Our regrets and our fears,
Our troubles and our worries.

Because life isn't about the past,
Don't gotta stay in this dream—
Life is about the present moment,
The future and our dreams.

I took a look in the mirror,
Took a look at myself.
I wondered why this was happenin'
Why I did what I did.

So many thoughts racing,

My hearts a-beating quick.
How could this even happen,
Happen to-o-o me-e-e-e?

God said to me, "Oh-h my child,
Why are you troubled so?
What's happened to your trust in me,
Your hope, your faith, and belief?

Don't you know I got your back?
Don't you see I know what's best?
I know you inside and out,
I know every bit of you!

Don't you worry my precious child,
All of this will work out in time,
I just want you to let go,
And let me take the wheel!"

So I said in reply, "Dear Jesus,
I wanna let go! I wanna be free!
Dear Jesus, please take this wheel
From me!

Take a hold of my life,
Of all my plans and dreams.
Hold onto my desires,
My wishes and sufferings!"

I'm gonna wake up today,

I'm gonna wake up tomorrow,
I'm gonna wake up the next day
And be free of this dream!

I'm gonna let go-o-o!
I'm gonna let go-o-o!
I'm gonna do whatever it is
That you ask of me.

I'm gonna shout, shout, shout for joy!
And thank you all day long!
For I know, that you know
What's best for me.

Help me to see,
Help me to wake up!
Help me to know
What you will have me do.

Oh-h-h God, I'm gonna let go!

Life is Complicating

Why is life so complicating?
Why do some things happen?
What's the reason for this?
Why is it so frustrating?

People change so often,
For better or for worse.
Some of them improve,
While others start to decline.

I'm so very disappointed,
Sad, distressed, and peeved.
I met someone whom I liked,
But really just as a friend.

The friendship seemed fine
Of course, this was the beginning.
Something ended up changing,
And I think it's for the worse.

This guy totally flipped
On our Catholic faith.
Got it off a youtube video,
And then an actual site.

He's so different now—
An entirely different person.
I feel we can't be friends,
The issue is too important.

It's so very frustrating
When you think things are okay;
When you think you've met a good guy;
When he has a sudden turnaround.

What's God's plan in this?
What's the reason for it?
I don't really understand,
I really don't know at all.

You make a friend,
And you lose a friend.
People come into your life,
And people go out of your life.
Sometimes if it'll be unhealthy,
If it'll cause much distress,
If it makes you angry and upset,
Then it's best to break a friendship.

Why have I not met
A good decent man?
A Godly man and more—
A man like St. Joseph?

I never seem to have
Many good experiences with men.
Honestly, it's no fun
When this all keeps happening.

Life has its ups and downs,
It certainly has its downs.
I have felt some ups too,
But recently feeling more downs.

All I really desire
Is to just raise a family.
I'm feeling like I'll quit,
Like I'll lose hope and give up.

They say I'm young still,
That I have plenty of time.
But is that really true?
We don't know for sure.

Does God want me
To actually raise a family?
How will I ever know?
When will I know?

Will I ever meet Mr. Right?
Will I meet Prince Charming?
Will I ever meet the man
Of my hopes and my dreams?

I don't know at all.
I only know this—
That life has the good and the bad,
And the unexpected always occurs.

I must trust in the Lord,
I must hope in Jesus.
I must have faith in Him,
And I can't ever give up.

Life

Life is a mess-
Well, it is sometimes.
Complex and frustrating,
Hard to even understand.

Why does it have to be?
When will anyone-
Ever understand me?
I am upset, feelin' lousy.

I lay down all my cares,
Sorrows, joys, concerns-
I pray and hope and try hard.
I want to be understood.

You know what's on my heart,
You know what's in my head,
You know how I feel,
And you know what to say.

I will not stop loving You.
And I very much love my luv;
I will always love my parents.
I mean what's there to be said?

Oh well, I don't know.
I know you have a plan.
You will guide me I'm sure,
And lead me onto the right path.

O Thorn of My Heart, O Rose of My Heart

O thorn of my heart,
Why hast thou-
My dear love,
Plagued me so?

You burn, throttle, warm
My weary, worn self-
A thorn from a rose
To pierce me through and through.

What have I done-
To deserve such cruelty?
What can be said
Of such suffering?

O thorn of my heart,
Answer my call, my plea,
And keep me from falling
Into the pits of misery.

But oh thorn,

Must you stay here long?
I entreat you to leave-
And farewell! Leave me be!
O thorn of my heart,
Turn into a lovely rose-
To warm me into radiant light
And keep me from harm's way.

O rose of my heart,
Love me, guide me, protect me,
Lead me not into danger,
And forever stay within me.

I thank thee Lord
For the thorn in my heart-
To suffer for all
And learn from my weakness.

I thank thee Lord
For the rose in my heart-
The triumph of good
And everlasting peace.

O thorn, wilt thou please
Change thyself to a rose?
And plague no other person
But myself alone.

But please if thou canst,
Let thorn turn to rose-
After all who have suffered
And find peace to give way.

O rose, you are my shield-
My soul rejoices with joy.
Don't ever leave me,
And lead me to the path of heavenly light.

Praise the Lord

I sing your praise,
Glorify You O Lord!
Wondrous is your name-
Almighty counsel and wisdom!

Your beauty is breath taking,
You shine like the sun,
For you are the Son of God-
The God-made man in flesh.

Your works are mighty-
Your love is sweet like honey.
Your compassion is abundant,
Your mercy-a flowing river.

I sit at your feet,
Gazing at your broken body.
How could humanity do it-
How could they be so cruel?

We put you to death-
Nailed you to a tree.
But you have the victory-
You conquered sin and death.

Now you reign victorious,
At the right hand of the Father-
With Mother Mary beside you,
And Joseph beside you too.

Shipwreck

Life is like a shipwreck;
The waves churn and crash,
Tossing you around in its waters
Like a helpless child who can't swim.

They try swallowing you whole;
When the rain starts to pour down,
And thunder and lightning commence—
It seems you might drown.

I feel at times in my life
That I've been thru many shipwrecks.
My plans are set to start,
But God decided to wreck them.

I'm treading thru dark waters,
Can't even see the bottom.
The ground seems so treacherous,
I'm scared I'll lose my balance.

I can't see what's coming,
Or even what is behind me;
Not what's under me either,
But only what is above.

Sometimes, life seems unreal.
I feel as if it's all a dream,
As if I do not exist, yet—
I sense that it is not a dream.

The waters grow colder and darker,
With each passing wave more violent than the last.
My ship tosses and turns,
And is battered by wind and rain.

I feel as I'm sinking,
Like Peter when he was walking on water.
I cry out to God for help,
But do not know if I was heard.

The noise of the waves is defeaning.
My head starts to ache,
My body grows cold and lifeless.
My strength has been cast out.
I wake up to the sunlight
Shining brightly upon me.
It seems I've been shipwrecked,
And somehow thrown to shore.

So many times in life,
This is how I've felt—
Like a ship tossed in the waves,
And scattered into many pieces.

I know there will always be
Such violent storms in life.
But I guess God pulls me through,
Even when I've felt stranded.

God sometimes wrecks your plans—
The plans you want to do.
He does so out of love,
For He doesn't want us hurt.

Our plans may wreck us,
Whether we know it or not.
They may push us away from God,
And be obstacles in growing closer to Him.

Thus, if God sees they're not good,
Not best for His little children,
He wrecks those plans that we had
To put His into action instead.

So many wrecks in my life,
So many plans disrupted.
God has saved me from trouble,
From further doom and disaster.

So, I carry on with life,
I continue to steer my ship.
The storms will come and go,
But I know that God has a plan for me.

Spiritual Battle

Here in this chapel
We sit, kneel, stand
In prayer and adoration,
In gratitude and thanksgiving.

All of us on a spiritual journey,
United in one Body and Church,
But on a different level,
Within our spiritual journey.

I see You in the monstrance,
So beautiful to behold-
Inside a lovely tabernacle,
So simple, yet so amazing.

I see You as Christ crucified
Hanging upon a tree,
With blood from your nail marks
And blood gushing from Your side.

You have won the war,
But we must fight the battles.
The demons try to drag us under,
Angels fight against them by our side.

I will not stop fighting my battles.
I will always keep pushing on,
For You have already been victorious-
You have already won the war.

Stuck

Day in and day out-
The same things occur.
No adventure or excitement,
Just a plain dull day.

What a rut we're in,
A plain, old-fashioned rut!
What are we going to do?
To escape from this muck?

Just pray, pray, pray-
And think about God.
Things that have been,
And things that will be true.

Be optimistic in your views-
No more whining and complaining.
Start each day anew
With a fresh perspective each morning.

Be joyous and kind,
And all things good.
Lend a caring hand,
And say, "How do you do?"

Just remember that you're precious,
Precious in God's loving eyes,
That you're a child of God,
And worth ever so much more.

The Cross

Bruised and beaten—
Whipped and scourged—
Tired and in anguish—
He still trodded on.

Sweat turned into blood,
Thorns pierced his skull;
His clothing clung to His skin,
His body was so disfigured.

He was determined to make it—
To complete His Father's will.
He kept on going on,
Even after falling three times.

The soldiers dragged off His garments—
So rough and callous they were,
That His skin came with them,
And His ribs were clearly so visible.

He was nailed to a tree
For our sins and offenses.
He wanted to embrace the Cross,
And he did it so freely.

Let this be a model
For us to embrace our crosses.
And remember you can turn to Him
When you feel most the weight of your cross.

Too Long

It's been too long
Since I've written a poem.
So, here I am now
Writing another poem.

I should've been writing
All throughout break,
But days and weeks passed,
Time just escaped me.

Break has lasted a while,
Way over one month.
But now it's already January,
Which means time for school.

It's also the new year,
But I don't make resolutions.
I just make it a goal
To improve and better myself.

I know of one thing
That I ought to work on-
I must deepen my prayer life,
Grow closer to God as well.

O may be excited for school-
Or maybe not, we'll see.
But just gotta go with it-
Gonna stick with the flow.

Troubling Times

In every age,
There are troubling times.
In every age,
There is much sorrow.

In every age,
There are wars and plagues.
And in every age,
There's death and dying.

However, it's not all doom and gloom-
For in every age,
There's laughter and joy,
Happiness and some peace.

When troubling times arise,
It's hard to see the positive.
When troubling times arise,
It's easy to see the negative.

When troubling times arise,
People will worry and have fear.
And when troubling times arise,
People allow fear to control them.

Does it have to be this way?
Should we let fear abound?
Does it have to be all sorrow?
Does it have to be all tears?

No, life doesn't have to be
Seen as all doom and gloom-
It doesn't have to be all sorrow.
It doesn't have to be all tears.

Fear is ever present,
But you don't have to bow to it.
You don't have to let it consume you,
You don't have to let it control you.

You must fight it-
Fear is your enemy!
A little fear is normal,
But not when it controls you.

We live in troubling times now,
There's no doubt about that.
But can we really say
That it's the worst of times?

Ukraine and Russia at war,
China and Taiwan maybe too;
The US and Canada with their own troubles,
Maybe it seems all hope is lost.

People are dying and hurting,
Freedoms and rights are at stake.
Our leaders are weak and greedy,
But the people are strong and loyal.

A country with patriots is a good thing,
The people won't back down.
They will put up a fight,
They won't ever give up.

Don't think all hope is lost.
Don't bow down to fear.
Don't be taken advantage of,
Don't let people manipulate you.

Do stand up and fight.
Do pray every day.
Do always have faith.
Do have trust in God.

God will not abandon you.
In times such as these
He is ever present,
Waiting for you to call on Him.

His Mother has outstretched arms,
Waiting to fold us in her mantle.
Mama Mary loves us all,
She wants no harm to befall us.

Although man has free will,
And the choices being made are not good,
We can use our free will
To choose the good and true.

Let us pray without ceasing,
Go about our day-
Don't worry about what you can't control,
Because God will take care of everything.

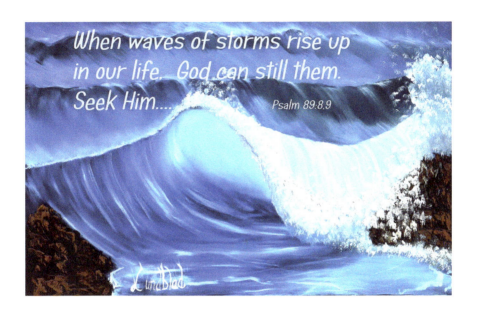

What am I Feeling?

There's a feeling that I have-
In my heart and my mind,
It's hard to describe
But I know that it's positive.

I feel content and happy,
Maybe even excited or joyful.
What words can explain
The feeling inside of me?

Exuberant, enthusiastic, hopeful?
Or maybe it's peace and calm?
The semester is closing slowly,
Maybe it's joy that I'll see my family.

Oh yes, I know now
That I feel gratitude-
Gratitude for everything that's happened,
Good, bad, neutral-what else!?

I feel ecstatic! That's the word!
Or is it…yes, I feel happy.
I could jump for joy
Or dance in my room!

Of course, deep down inside,
I know why I feel so light.
But it's between You, Lord and me-
Just our little secret.

When All Seems Hopeless (song)

When you think all around you, is falling to pieces and shattered
Life seems to become unreal, unworthy of being lived…
By Your servant
My senses are whirling, I feel broken and in despair
My sins are cast before me, before all ye heavenly bodies
I feel unforgiveable, I cry out to You Oh Lord, My God!
I beg for forgiveness, for peace and joy, laughter, harmony,
And rest in You my God.

When I feel broken, You build me up
When I am in despair, You comfort me
You take my sins upon Your shoulders, for you have forgiven me
You hear my cry, You hear me cry out for mercy!
You take me unto Your bosom, and You love me to the end.

You say, "My precious one, you known how much I love you
Dry those tears my daughter, lift up your face to me
I have a plan for you, a plan for you
Just trust in me, trust in me"

Oh Lord, I will trust in You!

Where Are You Taking Me

I feel so achy,
So lonely and depressed.
I'm really starving
For affirmation and hugs.

I am now sick,
And cold, and tired.
I'm frustrated and sad,
And very, very homesick.

I miss my home,
And my family too.
I just want to break down
And cry my tears out.

I've cried so much,
And still have more tears.
I feel so awful,
And I don't know what to do.

Why am I so vulnerable?
So hurt and so sad?
Why am I so sensitive?
So blue and so weak?

Where Lord are You taking me?
What direction will it be?
What have you in store for me-
For my life and my future?

I'm so lost and confused.
Yet somehow, I'm not.
I have a sense now
Of where I might be going.

I can only be patient and wait.
I can only have hope and pray.
I can be joyful and optimistic.
I can look forward to the future.

Have Mercy

Have mercy on us
Oh Lord, in our misery.
We are poor wretched creatures
Who rely on Your love and mercy.

Can You not see, my Lord,
What we are going through?
I know that You do,
But sometimes it's hard to believe.

You know, Oh Lord, our pain,
Our sorrows, joys, and grief.
I beseech You, my Savior,
Please hear our cries.

In our anxieties and frailties,
Please be with us.
In our pain and troubles,
Do not abandon us.

Guide us unto right paths,
Send down the Holy Spirit.
Protect us from all evil,
And deliver us from the evil one.

Amen.

God Knows Best

Sitting here in this pew,
Praying, wondering, hoping.
Staring at Jesus in the monstrance,
Seeing His radiant beauty.

I wonder about so many things,
Then I start to worry.
Oh, I must remind myself
That Jesus takes care of all.

Trust in the Lord! This I hear—
He knows what's best for me, for you.
He knows us well, me as a daughter; you, a son.
He is my Father, and He is your Father.

I love Him so much,
Not nearly enough as I should.
But I often wonder
What God has in store for me.

Rest assured, we needn't worry.
As long as we do our part,
God works on the details.
And remember that God knows best.

Seasonal Poems

April

It's the month of April.
A time of sunshine,
Rain, clouds, chilly morns-
So many colored flowers too.

It's a beautiful month,
Also, one of Easter-
Where You gave Yourself to us
Crucified on a tree.

But after all that suffering,
You rose from the dead.
Your body and soul glorified,
And sitting at our Father's right hand.

The sorrow your mother went through
Was certainly a mother's pain.
I can't begin to imagine
The joy she felt at seeing you alive.

The animals are out,
Flowers are blooming,
Buds on trees opening,
The days are getting warmer.

Thank you for this life,
It really is a gift-
Despite all the bad that happens,
Life is great overall.

Autumn

The leaves are falling-
They turn colors
Red, orange, yellow, purple
Like a rainbow in the sky.

The air is chilly;
The sky is still blue.
The wind whistles through the trees-
The sun still shines brightly.

Autumn is a beautiful season.
Maybe it's a time for change-
A time to reflect on the present
And look forward to the future.

Everything has a beginning-
Everything has an end.
It's just a continuous cycle
Of life, death, and re-birth.

Oh, but God had no beginning
And He has no end.
He exists everywhere and always
Past, present, future, infinity!

We have Autumn for a reason-
Don't take it for granted.
Enjoy those brightly colored leaves
And thank God for a wonderful day!

Changing Seasons

Bit by bit the petals fall-
All the way till the flower has died.
It wilts away and withers away
Till it can be seen no more.

One day in the spring-
It will rejuvenate.
The flower will thrive,
The petals shall blossom.

The fragrance is sweet;
The color has value.
Bees are attracted-
And the butterflies too.

Again, one day, the petals fall-
Bit by bit, all the way;
And the cycle continues on and on,
Till one day it'll be no more.

Advent

The season of waiting—
Of anticipating something bigger,
Is finally now upon us,
Bringing us hope and joy.

This season is the reason
For us to be at peace,
To be mindful and content
Of Christ's love for us.

Advent is a time of waiting
That teaches us much patience.
It's a season of prayer and penance,
And a season of good cheer.

It prepares us for
The most special of days.
And of course, that day is
The birth of our Savior, Jesus.

We should be so thankful
For such a precious gift;
For a wee babe who was born
In a stable in Bethlehem.

Christmas

Christmas season is drawing near,
It's a time of joy and cheer.
Of course, we should be jolly,
Humble and thankful as well.

It's a time to remember-
Of how wonderful life is.
Of the good times we've had,
And the friendships that we share.

Advent has come again-
A time of waiting and joy,
A time of patience and sacrifice,
To welcome a newborn babe.

Our Savior has been born,
The one who washes away our sins.
He was born in a manger,
In a cave, to our Mother Mary.

Born in poverty and died in poverty,
His life dedicated to the poor;
And now He reigns in Heaven,
For all of eternity.

Let's all remember this,
How Jesus was born in a manger-
On a cold, winter night,
As the most vulnerable of people.

Lent

Forty days and forty nights-
Oh! But wait good person,
Is it not a fact
That Sundays aren't included?

Yes, good sir that's true,
Sundays don't count in Lent.
But pray hear me out-
Tis good to sacrifice anyways.

Lent is a solemn time
Of fasting and abstinence;
Remembering Jesus' mission,
How he came to set us free.

He freed us from a bondage,
Our chains of prison-
He took our sins upon Himself,
And suffered a bloody death.

He loved us so tenderly,
He still loves us too.
So much to have wounds,
Five wounds of pierced love.

So, shall we remember
What the Holy Family suffered-
Of the love you gave us,
And the love you give today.

Summer

Summer should be fun!
A time of laughter and joy,
A time to spend with your family,
Fun moments that are memorable.

Everything is in full bloom.
Trees have green leaves-
Gardens are producing fruits-
The young frolick and play.

It's a season for trips,
For vacations and time alone.
A break for hard workers,
And a break from life's concerns.

Why is it that I feel
Something is different this time?
Are people, certain people
Trying to dampen our spirits?

Well, I won't listen to them!
We'll have so much fun;
I'll tend to the garden,
And do my classes.

Take walks, maybe swim, be free!
Time and life are precious;
Be fulfilling in your life,
And…take a trip to the beach!

New Life Poems

Darling Daughter

Oh, darling daughter,
We can't wait to see you.
Oh, darling daughter,
How we long to hold you tightly.

We have been waiting
Oh, so patiently
For your birth, darling,
To hold you in our arms.

God has been so gracious
To gift you to us.
For this we are grateful,
And thank God every day.

Oh, darling daughter,
You are so welcomed
Into this new world of ours.
God loves you, and we do too.

We will patiently wait
To hold your little hands,
To hear your little laughs,
And listen to your cries.

You are so loved,
And are very precious to us.
You help us complete
The family trinity.

We thank Heaven for you,
For such a precious gift.
Nothing could be sweeter
Than holding you in our arms.

Scattered Pieces

Life seems so hard,
So tough and complex.
The pieces fall to the ground,
Scattered and tossed by the wind.

Sometimes, it's depressing.
I guess I feel blue,
And maybe I feel lost,
And so confused and so broken.

God has said that-
Before we were in our mothers' wombs
That he knew us and created us
And already had plans for us.

He says, "You're the apple of my eye,
And I have great plans for you."
But what are those plans?
What is His will for me?

I feel blinded and stuck,
But I hold onto hope.
I won't give up now,
And won't ever give up.

God can pick up the scattered pieces
Of my broken life,
And put them back together
Till I'm made whole again.

The Lord Catches The Pieces Of Our Hearts And Heals The Broken Hearted

Second Chance

Oh, my Lord and Savior,
How much do I love You.
Words will never do justice
In expressing my love for You.

I've been falling short so much—
Recently life's been a mess.
I've been lax in my faith
And haven't visited You as I should.

I feel like a terrible person
For not spending enough time with You—
For you are my Creator and guide,
And You are the reason I'm still alive,

I've been so down and depressed lately,
My spiritual life has been shattered.
There seems to be no stability
And no consistency in life itself.

My jobs come and go very often,
School life is such a wreck.
I'm such a stupid fool
To think I could do anything myself.

You should be and are my everything.
You are the reason I can breathe,
You are the reason I wake in the morning.
So, there must be a reason I still exist.

Dear God, I need help!
Please give me a second chance!
I want to be wild and free
Like a wild horse that knows no bounds!

I ask, I beg, I plead at thy feet
For assistance in all my endeavors.
Please show me where to go,
What to do, speak, and say.

Please strengthen me every day;
Be my shepherd every night.
Guard me from the snares of sin,
And from the wolves that may surround me.

Please uplift my downtrodden spirit;
Give me joy, patience, peace, and courage.
Help me to see You in others,
And others to see You in me.

Help me form Godly friendships,
Bring me friends who will help me through
All the trials and terrors of this life,
And most of all, who will help me attain eternal life.

Thank You God for my life,
For my family, friends, for You.
I ask again, dear Jesus,
Please give me a second chance.

Welcome Baby Boy!

Welcome baby boy
To this new world of yours!
How strange it will seem
When you first open your eyes!

So many shapes and sizes,
And so many colors.
All these eyes staring at you—
Who are these people?

Your mom and dad
Are pumped to see you—
To hear your cries and laughs,
And have so many cuddles.

That little smile you'll give,
That tiny laugh that will burst forth,
And those small little fists and kicks
Are so much to treasure.

One of the most precious gifts God gives
Is in the form of a tiny human being.
Oh, what joy it that we have
To witness the birth of a child!

Oh, my dear little one, dear baby boy,
Mommy and Daddy can't wait to hold you in their arms.
They'll wait patiently for that day to come
When they will welcome you into their world.

Love Poems

Best Mom Ever

The month of May
Has finally drawn near.
The showers pour down-
The flowers spring up.

Baby animals everywhere
Fritter all about.
Their mommies stand by-
Making sure all is going fine.

There is a day in May
That celebrates all mothers-
The time that they sacrifice,
And the work that they do.

There is a woman
Who always makes my day;
She is most amazing and clever,
Patient, kind, and calm.

My mom is special-
Best mom ever alive on earth.
She cares for me so much-
In my sickness and my health.

She deserves so much more,
More than I can give.
How can I say thanks?
How can I show my gratitude?

Mom, you're the best ever!
You make me laugh and cry!
You help me with my struggles,
And listen to my heartaches.

Thanks so much for everything-
For being an awesome mom.
You're loved by all of us and God,
You're so beautiful, always.

I'm blessed to have a woman
So ready to be my mom.
You do so much already-
It's time you take a break.

I know you love us all,
We all love you too!
Just be the amazing woman you are,
And I promise there'll be no regrets.

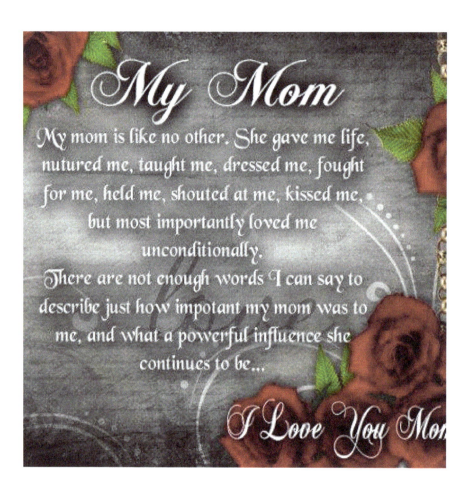

Mama, I Love You

There have been times
That I've taken you for granted,
And there have been times
That I didn't understand you.

I don't really know
If I've been the best daughter,
But I will say this:
"I'm so happy you're my mom."

I know I've been rude,
I know I've talked back,
I know I've cried for help,
But didn't take your advice.

I'm sorry for all the heartache
That I have ever caused you.
You're one awesome mom,
And only deserve the best!

I pray to be a better daughter,
To be there for you always.
You've always been here for me,
In good times and bad.

Thank you so much again
For being my mom for another year.
I'm so grateful God gave you to me,
And I promise to become a better daughter.

I don't have a gift,
No candles, soap, nothing like that—
But what I do have to give
Is my love as a devoted daughter.

Mama, I love you so much!
You'll always be in my heart.
I will always be thankful
For your presence in my life.

Thank you, God, for my mom,
Thank you, God, for my life.
Thank you, God, for our lives together,
And thank you God for the days to come.

To My Mother

Oh mother, dear mother-
There's so much to say!
You do so much for me
And always are there when needed.

You do what moms know best-
Like care for sick children,
Clean and sweep the house,
And cook delicious meals!

It's hard to even put
Everything into words.
I appreciate all you do,
Even if I don't show it.

You really do inspire me,
In many different ways-
And I do look up to you,
Every single day.

Your voice is in my head-
Day in and day out;
Maybe that's exaggerating,
But you get the point.

I remember what you tell me-
Rules and old sayings.
I hear you when I'm struggling,
When I feel blue and am away from home.

So, I just wanted to say-
Thanks from the bottom of my heart.
Thanks for what you do,
And thanks for being my mom.

Thanks for giving me life,
For being around when I needed you,
For hearing me out when I needed to talk,
And even just for your presence.

We've had a million laughs,
We've had times when we grieved,
We've had times when we quibbled,
And we've had times when we prayed.

I can't imagine life without you,
Well, I can but it's hard.
You have done so much for us,
And I look forward to more years to come.

So, once again thank you.
I love you so much.
Thanks for all that you do,
And all that you will do.

Mothers

Dear mothers, dear mothers,
We wish to thank you
For being our mothers
And a gift to us.

You do so much
In this world of ours.
The sacrifices you make
Do not go unnoticed.

To some you are nothing,
And others ignore you.
But to God you're so special,
So, you're special to me.

The angels in Heaven
May be jealous of you,
For they can't have the gift
Of motherhood as you do.

You are our heroes!
You work full-time,
All day, every day, and every night
With no time for breaks or rest.

But the rewards are amazing—
From watching your unborn baby grow,
To giving birth and caring for your little one,
And keeping house while raising your family.

You hear a cry at 3am—
Time to feed the baby.
You hear yells from a room—
Time to stop that fighting.

Always busy, always serving,
Let it be known to you—
You are so loved and appreciated,
In my eyes, you're a hero!

So, thank you for being here,
In the good times and bad.
Thank God you're here,
And keep up that amazingness!

My Love for Him

My love for him is great-
No mushy feelings,
No butterflies in the stomach-
None of that nonsense.

Rather something else,
Self-sacrificing love.
Passion, intimacy, commitment
And a bond stronger than ever.

Years came by before
This love was discovered.
A hundred percent positive
About this being true love.

I must hope-can't despair
So far we seem to be,
Yet so close-
That love has brought to me.

I miss him so much,
Oh, it's ever so painful
To be separated from him,
But I'm happy to follow God's will.

Step by Step

Oh, how I love you!
I know you love me too.
One day it'll happen-
The day that we wed.

Of course, it must be-
Taken step by step.
I mean that's the way-
The way it should be.

So, first we must be court-
Just talk and have fun.
Go out with friends-
And spend time with family.

Next, we shall date-
But it must be chaste.
We can spend time together,
Even by ourselves!

We ought to pray together,
Go to Mass as well.
Watch family shows,
And talk of future family.

Finally, we're engaged!
Take our nuptial classes.
Wait for a min 6 months-
Then we shall marry!

To My Dad

This is to someone special-
I am so grateful to him.
I may not act like it,
And at times, I take him for granted.

Thank you for raising me,
For teaching me what I know.
For spending time with me,
And being there when I needed it.

There comes a time though
When a daughter starts to blossom,
Step by step she matures,
And soon one day, a full woman.

The time will come when-
A man wants to court her.
He will ask you so for permission,
For he honors her parents.

She hopes you say yes,
For one day she shall marry.
You will walk her down the aisle,
And give her away to another.

For now I say thank you!
I look forward to time spent
Together in future years.
I love you a lot! Thanks dad!

To My Future Spouse

My dear beloved,
I have waited a long time
To finally meet
The man God has sent to me.

I don't know his name,
Nor the color of his eyes,
Nor the shade of his hair,
Or whether he has wide set eyes.

I pray that he's faithful,
That he loves me through and through.
He'll look me in the eyes and say-
"I love you very dearly."

I pray we're both chaste and pure,
We'll save all that we have
To give to each other-
On that most precious night of nights.

We'll say our vows meaningfully,
Remembering our promises,
To love each other till the end,
Till death do us part.

Our love will then bear fruit,
Many blessings to come.
Hopefully many children shall come,
From the bond we share so tenderly.

You are the one I have loved,
Loved most after loving God.
But I'll continue to wait,
For as long as the setting sun.

To My Love

Oh, my darling!
How much I love you!
Words can't express-
How I feel for you.

I don't know what to say-
My heart yearns for you.
I know I must be patient,
The time will come soon.

I just want to hug you,
To hold your hand in mine.
To see you face to face-
To press my lips to yours. (in marriage)

I wonder when this will be-
When will it happen?
Will we get a chance
To ever be together?

I hope we meet soon,
But all in God's timing.
Everything will be fine,
I know it'll work out.

I can't wait to see you,
To be held in your arms.
I love you very much,
And I know you love me too.

When I'm With You

Every time I think of you,
Every moment I am with you,
Every second I stare into your eyes,
My heart skips a beat.

So many days have gone by
When I thought I'd lose hope.
So many hours ticked by
And not even fast enough.

I really thought this was it,
That there was no one out there.
I wondered just who it was
That God may have in store for me.

I gave up looking and searching,
I was too worn out.
My heart ached all over
From past hurt and rejection.

All that was really certain
Was that uncertainty abounded—
Everywhere and at every time,
Nothing could I be certain of.

The time came when I felt torn,
Trying to mend my heart again.
I prayed to Jesus to pick up these pieces
And to make my heart whole again.

Only Jesus can complete me,
That much I knew.
Only Jesus can mend this heart
That was broken into pieces.

I gave my heart to Him
Where I knew it'd be safe.
He started healing my heart
By pouring out His perfect love.

However, little did I know
That a surprise was in store.
Just when I figured all was lost
You showed up in my life.

I was very guarded at first,
Not trusting as I should.
I didn't want to go through
Any more heartbreak and tears.

But Jesus saw fit to take my heart,
Having mended it whole again,
And gave it to you to care for,
To love, honor, and respect.

Jesus opened my heart up again,
Told me not to be afraid.
Life was not what it seemed,
All hope was not lost.

Once you came into my life,
And my heart opened up,
I saw that it was true—
That you would not hurt me.

My heart started to skip a beat
Whenever we were together.
Whenever we were with friends,
I always noticed when you'd arrive.

When we are together,
I see the look in your eyes.
That says it all to me—
Tender warmth, understanding, and trust.

You did not rush me or push me,
But allowed me to open up gradually.
It wasn't long before I knew
That I was in love with you.

One day you took me aside,
And held my hands so gently.
Looking into my eyes, you said to me
That you love me for who I am.

That was the day we both knew
That God had planned for us.
All those past experiences and hurt
Prepared us to be with each other.

God knows we love Him above all,
And each other after Him.
But let me just say it again,
When I'm with you, my heart skips a beat.

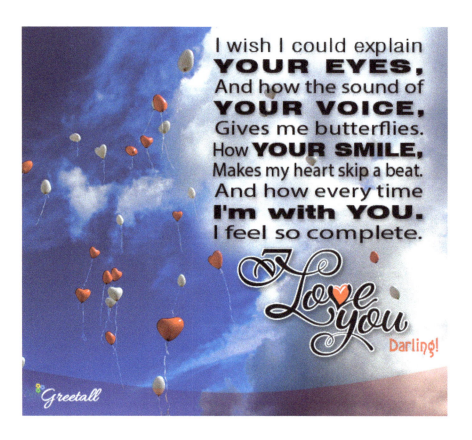

My First Love

I count the stars at night,
Or rather, I can try.
But they are so vast,
They seem to be infinite.

I see the sun in its glory
And feel its warmth on my face.
Its beauty is surpassing,
And its brightness is amazing.

The universe is so grand
With the earth and all its wonders,
All in existence at once,
And it's all so very good.

As broken as we are
God still loves us—
For He gave us the universe,
The earth and all its beauty.

We have marred ourselves,
Hurt ourselves and hurt others;
But Jesus helps to pick us up
And pushes us to go onward.

Jesus is our first Love;
Jesus is my first Love.
My life will be centered around Him,
My very existence is for Him.

I can never love Him as I should,
But try all the more.
Mi love Him through other people,
And through Mass and adoration.

God, have mercy on us, please,
And bring souls closer to You.
Help me to love everyone,
And to plant the seeds of conversion.

You are my first Love,
And will always be first.
You dance with me in this life,
Always pulling and keeping me close.

I wish everyone loved You like this,
As their first and foremost Love.
Nothing is more important
Than the Love between us and You.

Please dance with me
Till You see fit to send
A man to me in marriage
Who loves You as much as I do.

You, Lord, must be his first Love,
And at the center of his life.
His life must revolve around You,

As much as is humanly possible.

I sense that you might send
Such a man to me.
But only You know for sure,
And till then, You'll dance with me.

You know me more than I know myself,
And more than I know You.
So, help me to better know You,
To love and serve You with all my being.

Jesus is here for me,
And He is there for you too.
He is my first Love,
And should be your first Love too.

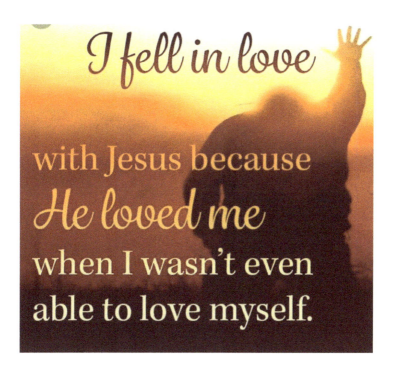

I fell in love with Jesus because He loved me when I wasn't even able to love myself.

Grief Poems

A Mother's Sorrow

A mother's sorrow is real;
She watches her child die,
Or hears about her child's death-
And the tears flow like a fountain.

The hardest thing for a mother-
The hardest thing in her life-
Is to see and hear of the death of her child,
Something no mother should have to bear.

Women are strong creatures.
They bear and raise their children
With so much loving care,
And such tender embraces.

No matter how the child turns out,
His mother will always love him.
However long he tries her patience,
She will endure it all just for him.

This is a sacrificial love-
A love that can bring joy,
But can also bring pain as well,
For it calls mothers to endure much suffering.

Mama Mary knows how you feel.
She herself knows pain and suffering-
For she saw her only Son
Hanging upon a tree.

Mama Mary loved Jesus so much.
She bore him and raised Him,
Cared for Him and loved Him,
And was willing to take her part in His passion.

She gave up her only Son,
So that we all would live.
She watched Him be tortured and killed-
Her heart was pierced with a lance.

But Mama Mary did it for us!
She loves us all so tenderly.
She enfolds us in her mantle,
And cares for us every day.

She knows what all mothers go through.
She knows what you're suffering.
She shares in all you're going through,
For she too has a mother's heart.

But do not grieve for long,
For Mary has him at her side.
She will care for your son,
Till one day, you both meet again.

A New Life

Words cannot express
The sadness in our hearts;
The pain that we feel,
And the tears that we shed.

We treasure your life on earth,
The fun memories we have.
All the cares and setbacks,
Joys, sorrows, and fun times.

But God took you away,
You lived a well-lived life.
It was time for you to go,
To leave and be with our Savior.

I'm not sure why it was now,
Only God can answer that.
But you will always remain in me,
In my heart, soul, memories.

We love you so dearly,
And know you are in Heaven.
Starting a wonderful new life,
With your heavenly family.

Please guide us into life,
Pray for us, protect us-
Till we meet again
In the land of eternity.

A Story

Once upon a time,
There lived a young man
Who met a young woman,
And two years later were married.

Before anyone knew it,
They had a daughter,
And next thing you know,
They had two sons.

Life wasn't without its trials,
For that couple bore much pain.
The woman had some miscarriages
Which caused great distress.

The woman had been a single mother,
But was also strong and brave.
The man did his best
To help raise her son.

Thus, the number of children
That the couple raised
Turned out to be four—
Oh, what glorious days.

There came the day when
The oldest entered marriage,
And before the blink of an eye,
Were raising six children.

The couple was always proud
Of these beautiful grandchildren.
The other children were still growing,
And becoming a wild bunch of kids.

Somehow or other, the couple survived.
The girl graduated high school,
And then graduated college.
Her father was proud of her.

College wasn't without
All its trials and tribulations.
His daughter was struggling
And there came emails galore.

Her father did what he could
To help his only daughter.
He even traveled to Italy
When she suffered from her appendix.

But she pulled through college,
With her father always there.
She could count on him
To help her through it all.

The next son graduated
From high school too.
He entered college,
And his dad was proud of him.

The youngest still in high school
Hasn't graduated yet.
But dad was proud of him,
And everything he did.

We may never know the reason
For what happened next.
It was the beginning of 2023
When dad was called home.

He knew many people,
Touched so many lives.
Many people touched him,
Of that I am sure.

His faith was important
Up to his death.
God prepared his soul
For its time to come home.

It was sudden and unexpected,
And shocked many people.
His daughter couldn't believe it,
Their father was gone.

I know dad loved us,
And will always love us.
He will always be with us,
In our hearts and memories.

Sometimes I do wish
I could wake up from this,
And call it a nightmare,
Which is what it is.

However, I do realize
That dad is now truly happy.
Nothing could get him
To leave Heaven for earth.

It's best he is there,
And can help us continue life.
I need all the help I can get,
For I'm a lot to handle.

I will miss him a lot,
I will cry a lot.
But that's okay, I know.
It is normal to grieve.

I look forward to the day
When I can see him again.
But until that time comes,
We must persevere in life.

Have no fear mother,
Have no fear, my brothers.
Dad's happy where he is,
And loves us all the more.

Confusion

My sorrow is real-
Lifelike, vivid, detailed.
The time came so suddenly,
A rushing storm so quick.

The burst of emotions I feel-
Sorrow, fear, joy, anguish, happiness
Doesn't account for half of it,
Or even the way I feel now.

I can't believe it even now,
I am stuck listening to-
Weird strange songs,
But another story that will be.

College is hard-
I miss my life-
My family my friends, my home;
Normal as it was, it was very good.

I want to cry, cry all night-
Cry myself to sleep.
But I know I am maturing,
As slow a process it seems to me.

I know there are plans,
Plans God has for me,
Plans I may not know,
But I'll trust in Him forevermore.

Dear Daddy

Dear daddy, I miss you so—
Your smile and laughter,
Your jokes and humor,
Even your receding hairline.

We had our ups and downs,
Our squibbles and our squabbles.
But we had good times,
Which are memories to be cherished.

You died so suddenly,
No one expected it at all.
I am beyond shocked,
And shocked is an understatement.

I really love you and miss you.
Only God knows what happened.
He has a reason for all this,
For why you left when you did.

Life seems so depressing now,
I can barely write.
The tears fall like waterfalls,
And maybe will never stop.

You touched people's lives,
That I can now see.
You were proud of me too,
That I never knew.

Daddy, tell me you're fine,
That you're doing just dandy.
Give me a sign please
That all will be fine.

Give us all strength and courage,
Perseverance to fight on.
Help me not to lose my faith,
And not to be mad at God.

Gone

Well this time it happened-
I knew it was coming.
My hopes are bashed,
My dreams are gone.

I feel lonely, awful-
I did love him so!
He loved me too-
Guess it's not meant to be.

We had such fun hopes and dreams;
Live on a farm, be together.
But now it's all gone,
Won't ever happen now.

I don't really understand.
I cry so much now.
It was so deep and intimate,
We hoped it'd work out.

Life goes on though-
When God closes a door-
He opens a window.
Though I am doubtful for now.

Why did it happen?
Who really knows?
Guess I must go on-
I must look towards the future!

I Don't Understand

Day after day passes by.
Morning comes and the evening comes
Over and over again,
Until it becomes depressing.

Sometimes life seems so weary,
So mundane and so dull.
I don't really understand it—
Why it can feel this way.

At times I feel happy,
And at times I feel joyful.
But there are times I feel sad,
And times when life seems a mess.

Why do people so often
Come in and out of my life?
Why do relationships always
Have to come to an end?

I wish I had a friend
That would always be here for me,
And yes, I know Jesus does that,
But it's not the same for me.

I need a human shoulder
To cry on and rest my head against.
I need someone to cheer me on,
Who will persevere, even when times are tough.

People just aren't like that.
They come and go at will.
They're here when times are swell,
And disappear when times get rough.

I want to know I'm loved,
That someone feels loved by me.
I wish I could make a difference,
In the life of some other person.

I don't feel I touch people's lives,
That I ever make a difference.
I know people might say otherwise,
But that's very hard to believe.

Sometimes I feel like punching myself
For all the things I've done.
Memories flash before me,
And life does a flip-flop.

So many things are triggers,
Of my failings in life.
And when those failings arise,
I feel so scared and helpless.

I've been manipulated before,
Accused of things I didn't do.
Emotionally toyed with it seems,
And not respected as a young woman.

I've been exposed to things
That robbed me of my youth.
My innocence disappeared,
My purity seemed to flee.

I still have wounds from this,
Wounds that won't heal.
I know forgiveness is vital,
But somehow, I can't forgive myself.

People can say what they want,
It doesn't matter to me.
But one thing I know for sure—
This is my cross to bear.

Life seems like it's falling apart
At different times in life.
But I know when that happens
Life is really falling into place.

Of course, I feel something
Is not as it should be.
Or rather should I say
That I'm missing something in my life.

I guess God will let me know
All in good timing.
Until that time comes,
I must continue on with life.

Life is Tough

Why do I feel
So sad, lonely, depressed-
Life is so complicated and tough,
So full of wounds and scars.

I don't even know
How long to push on;
How far I can go
Before I conk out.

I can do nothing myself,
But only through You Lord
Can I do anything
For all things are possible through you.

Please take away
These heart's desires of mine
To marry and raise a family
Till the time is right.

When that time comes,
Show him to me,
Show me to him,
And let us know what you will.

I feel like giving up
From my past experiences.
But I know that I must
Continue to fight, move on.

Life is rocky and bumpy,
Full of tears and sadness,
But also, joy and happiness.
Life is a mix of emotions.

So, I thank God
For everything that befalls me,
And I will always praise Him
Till the end of time.

Looking Back

Sometimes we wonder
Why a loved one left so quickly.
Why God called them to home
With no time to say goodbye.

So many years spent
Laughing till we cried,
And so much time spent
In just being able to love you.

After living our lives together,
For the years that we did,
It was time for someone to go—
It was time for you.

Why God called you, not me
I'll never know.
But life continues on,
And I know I'll see you soon.

God blessed us abundantly
With many married years.
Children came along,
And then grandchildren too.

We were there for each other
Through the best of times.
And we stuck it out together
When times became tough.

God sent you to me,
To be in my life through marriage.
And he has seen fit now
To call you back home.

I will always cherish
Those years together,
Those times of joy,
And times of sorrow.

So, farewell for now.
I shall live on.
Life will continue onwards
Until we meet again.

I thank God for everything
That He's blessed me with.
I know you're with Him now,
And that's good enough for me.

𝓘 was supposed to spend the rest
of my life with you
And then I realized… you spent the
rest of your life with me
I smile because I know you loved me
till the day you went away
And will keep loving me…
till the day we're together again.

Lost Loved Ones

There are so many memories
That we hold very dear,
Of loved ones gone before us—
Their laughs, cries, and tears.

They remain within us,
In our hearts and our minds.
We'll never forget them,
And never stop praying.

We mustn't mourn forever,
They wouldn't want that.
They'd want us to be happy,
Filled with tears of joy.

When we are struggling,
Let us pray to them.
They would be excited
To intercede for us.

This life isn't the end.
It doesn't stop here.
It's merely a journey,
And it's only the beginning.

The day will come soon
When we'll see them again.
But don't rush it, my friends,
For that could be a disaster.

We will be called home
When our hearts are ready.
God is working within them,
And He knows when it will be time.

Motivation

When dad was alive,
I had motivation.
Life was better it seems,
And more fulfilling.

Now dad is gone,
And I feel depressed.
I have little motivation,
And life is a mess.

I still live life though,
Do all my activities.
I don't have a job now
Which is very frustrating.

I don't think I want one
Since I don't have much talent.
But a job is necessary
To earn and save up.

I just feel that
Life isn't as great.
When dad left,
A piece of me left too.

I pray Jesus will help
To bring me motivation.
Courage and fortitude too,
Whatever else I lack.

I guess Dad will help
In his own little way.
But it sure isn't the same,
When he's not physically here.

Frankly, I'll admit
That I just wanna go.
Leave here for heaven,
Leave all this behind.

But God still has plans,
And I'm still here living.
So, I'm not ready to leave,
There's more work to be done.

I just wanna raise
A family sometime soon.
Care for a husband,
And many children too.

God has His timing,
So, things will fall into place.
I just have to be patient,
And accept all with an embrace.

Tears

A cry of distress
And a cry of sorrow
Have breached the silence
And reached my ears.

The tears fall down
In a generous amount.
The cries that come forth
Seem to be that of sorrow and grief.

I see the woman
While I'm in the chapel,
Praying ceaselessly, yet—
Her tears flow like a fountain.

I pray whatever it is,
That whatever is bothering her,
Will melt away like snow
And calmness will enter its place.

I pray for her peace of mind,
For her soul to be comforted.
For Mama Mary to care for her,
For Jesus to console her.

I don't know what her grief is,
What sorrow has befallen her,
What I do know is that she's human,
And is in need of love and comfort.

I didn't get to hug her,
Go over and see what's happening.
All I was able to do
Was to write this poem for her.

I see she's left and gone,
A little quieter than before.
I hope she is all right,
That she's found some peace of mind.

I pray for her tonight,
And entrust her to Mary.
I pray that her anxieties
Will turn into joys.

I'll wonder what was going on,
What was causing those tears,
But that's between her and God,
And I just need to pray.

School Poems

A Month of School

Well, now I can't believe it!
It's end of week four!
That is so exciting-
A month has already gone by!

The food is okay though,
Starting to taste a little bland.
But I know I really shouldn't
Complain about anything.

The ice cream is really good,
Sometimes the meat is too.
I love their chocolate milk,
And sweet tea hits the spot.

The dorm is nice, the room too.
My bed is very comfy.
The room is cooling off,
Not so humid anymore.

Of course, I'm excited
As usual for break again.
So, there's some motivation
To excel in all I do.

Remember to be grateful-
Praise God for all blessings
And thank God for all that happens
Because you're lucky to be here in person.

Midterms

Has it been six weeks?
Already a month and a half!
I know it's hard to believe-
Thank God the weeks fly by.

Misterm are upon us-
I'm sure everyone is happy.
Totally we're jumping up and down,
Shouting for joy for exams.

No, really, I'm stressed.
The semester has been crazy.
It seems all I do is work;
Eat work, sleep, and over again.

At least it's a routine,
And break will soon be here.
But I have to do well now,
On all these upcoming exams.

I pray I do well,
And that everyone does well.
Say a prayer for us,
I'll say a prayer for you.

Bye for now, farewell!
Adieu till I write again!
Hope for the best for these exams,
Let's say I'm ready for a rest!

Mindblowing

I'm going to say something,
That will blow your mind!
Or maybe it'll not be
That surprising at all.

We're halfway through the semester!
Isn't that plain exciting?!
Part way though Lent-
Easter will be here soon!

I'm looking forward to family,
To going home for break.
School has been crazy,
Overwhelming with stress.

I know I feel drained,
And sometimes I'm depressed,
Lonely, distressed, fatigued…
Maybe I'm too negative.

I will be more positive,
Patient, trusting, hopeful,
Looking forward to break and summer,
And being grateful for God's blessings.

Thank you, Lord, for my life,
For my family, friends, boyfriend.
God knows how much that I love them.
I love him and I love Jesus most of all!

One Crazy Week

This week has been tough-
So much work to do,
So many classes,
And not enough time for it all.

I was a little panicked
Since not all my hours
Were going to be met, but-
The professor reassured me.

I'm sure things will be fine.
I hope get all A's,
Maybe some B exceptions,
I just want to do well this semester.

It's been crazy for sure-
So many things happening,
Like getting strep and colds,
And having drama in your life.

Life has been busy.
I have been really busy.
Sometimes I'm not sure
If I'm dreaming or am in reality.

At times, life seems so unreal.
One day goes into the next.
Days just all run into each other,
And it seems life one large day.

What surprises me most
Is how I got here.
A senior, last semester, in college,
And here at Franciscan.

A girl, or woman now,
Studying clinical psychology,
With an internship at a school,
Working with mischievous little kids.

This was all unexpected.
Having an ex wasn't expected.
I just never know what'll happen,
Or what God has in store for me next.

Stressed Out

So stressed out,
Who knows why?
Could be my classes,
Or maybe even lessons.

Whatever it is,
I must resolve.
I must relax,
And forget my troubles.

But oh! I want to cry!
I feel so frustrated,
Tests, essays, quizzes,
And ever so much more!

What to do about riding,
And all the lessons galore.
What to buy for shows-
And how I've no idea.

Oh, it costs so much.
Prices are so high!
But I shall manage somehow,
And trust in God evermore.

The End is Near

The end is near-
I can't believe it!
The weeks fly by
And finals are coming.

The end of winter-
Is finally here.
Spring has come-
The time of re-birth.

The end to snow-
The beginning of rain.
What follows rain
But the shining sun!

I see a rainbow-
Where does it end?
What will I find-
Besides a pot of gold?

I go to the end
And I find-
Beautiful green grass
And colorful flowers.

Of course, some say
That it's the end.
But I say that-
"It's just the beginning!!"

Time for School

School has now begun.
Students are excited
To meet and see each other
And to start new classes.

Some are here as new students,
Some are returning students,
Some have just transferred,
And others are only commuters.

I am here now,
As a returning student.
Although I was new before,
I am not anymore.

But my brother is here,
And that is good for sure.
But I do miss my family,
And my home, bed, everything.

I know I need to pray,
Look at the future, don't look back;
Take opportunities placed before me-
And strive to make new friends.

I will always miss home,
But I must get to know
The people here and make friends,
Become independent-it'll be okay.

Two Months-Maybe More?

Okay, it has been two months.
No-it has been more than that!
Wow, I can't believe it-
I guess time does fly.

I'm glad it's nearing the end,
Closer and closer we get.
It's close to the end of October,
Then it'll be November.

The semester has been rough,
Stressful and challenging for sure.
Lots of school work and exams,
Papers, quizzes, projects-yay.

But soon it'll be Thanksgiving,
Then we will have a break.
Of course, we have to study,
Cause exams are right afterwards.

My family will come up here,
Jacob and I will stay on campus.
Many students will be here-yes,
Excited for the semester to end.

Well, I'm glad there's one month left.
Actually, a little more than a month.
We'll fight through it together!
I know that we can do this!

Miscellaneous Poems

Loving Face

When I look at you,
I see your face.
What can I say?
Except it's as beautiful as lace.

Your dark brown hair
Shines like the sun.
Your shining smile
Reminds me that you're so much fun.

Your loving eyes are
So beautiful to behold.
Those daring brown eyes,
Is what makes you so bold.

Your marvelous beauty
Shines over your face;
But so does your soul-
They're both beautiful as lace.

A Storm

A storm is brewing—
Brewing fast on the horizon.
The clouds gather together,
They darken to an intense color.

The sky looks angry,
It booms out thunder;
The lightning flashes quickly,
And then the rains come down.

Everything seems gloomy,
The storm is relentless—
Wetting everything in its path
And striking trees where it may.

Yes, the trees totter—
They are battered by the wind.
The sun has gone away,
And no one is outside to play.

But only for a while
Is the storm a ravaging beast—
For the rains lessen,
And the winds calm.

The thunder becomes distant,
The lightning will soon be gone.
The clouds will disperse,
And the sun will break through strong.

So again the story goes,
The sun comes out, then goes back in.
Clouds darken the sky-
And the ravaging beast, a menace to all,
Will return once again.

Accepting Change

There's a time in life
When a person matures,
When the past is the past,
And the future has yet to come.

The present moment
Is what's focused on.
We must not live
In our past or future.

Now in my life's journey,
I've come to a fork in the road.
I can live in the past and worry,
Or accept reality and move on.

I have come to realize
That people walk into your life,
For good reasons that God knows,
But can be taken away as well.

It's hard to deal with,
I've struggled in facing reality,
That God sent two people to me,
Only now to take them away.

I was best friends with two girls,
Friends we were in high school,
Even the beginning of college,
And into sophomore year.

But alas, my heart cries out!
To recall all the good times
Can be painful and hard,
Sad, joyful, happy, and crying.

It makes me realize
That they were in my life for a reason,
That the time has now come
For us to move on.

I am so thankful
For the times we shared together.
We had so much fun,
And many talks, laughter, and tears.

They helped me through rough times,
The rough patches in my life.
They were there for me,
When I needed them most.

Now we are distant-
Who knows if we are friends.
I guess I've been angry,
Feeling hurt and upset.

For such a long time now,
I've wondered about it all,
About our relationship,
And what will happen next.

I have felt they're disinterested,
Not wanting to be friends.
And many times, I've asked
"Do they even still care?"

I know it's not a mystery,
I've reflected on this a lot-
As to why we're close no more,
And don't talk or visit as before.

We've hit that part in life
Where we'll go our separate ways.
Now it's time for a change,
To make new friends and have fun.

I wish them all the best
In their whole lives' endeavors,
Blessings in all they do,
And hope for a bright future.

I have grown so much
Throughout the years together.
I've learned so much too,
It was such a grand time.

But now I say goodbye,
I'm not holding back,
Won't hold onto the past,
Or be angry and upset.

I say farewell today,
To these girls who helped me a lot.
And I will look forward to the future,
To exciting days ahead.

The future is uncertain,
I don't know who I'll meet-
Who I'll befriend,
And who will be a best friend.

I only know this-
That God has a plan for me,
That He loves me very much.
He's always looking out for me and will for all eternity.

Everyone goes through change.
It's inevitable and everywhere.
We must accept the reality of change,
And continue with life as usual.

P.S. You'll be relieved that you did!

"**Friendship** is not finding **gold or silver** among the rocks **of life.** It is accepting each other as **coal** until **diamonds** are formed with time."

Corona Virus   (song)

I am the corona virus,
People are scared of me
Just by sight and thought.
Gosh what fun I have!

So, here's a little dilly
That I made up for you
To show just how silly
What people seem to do!

"I am the co-ro-na vi-i-rus who won't do anything,
All I do is jump around, I spread my germs fairly qui-ick-ly,
To people all around! All who see me are scared away, they shop and stockpile up! Boy, oh boy I cause good havoc! But one day, I shall die!!"

That's my dilly to you,
Sing it along if you want,
Any tune fits and it's MY honor
To hear people pay so much attention

TO ME!!!

Day by Day

I try to take it-
Day by day.
I try to be calm
Day by day.

I don't want to be stressed
Or hurt or worried,
But it'll come anyways
And I must be prepared.

Things happen for a reason,
Life goes on-
It seems so complex,
So hard and so frustrating.

Sometimes I am exhausted-
At times I feel sick;
I get lonely and depressed,
Tired, bored, and irritated.

There have been good things,
I should focus on that.
I ought not to be selfish
And should take things as they are.

Life will go on-
Days, weeks, months will pass by;
Be grateful for the little things
And know how blest you really are.

Friendship

I don't feel worth it-
To have so many friends.
I don't deserve them-
I am very wretched.

But friends are vital.
True friends stick with you;
They love you and care for you-
They share your tears and smiles.

They also tell you truths,
If you're doing wrong.
They caution you and protect you,
They know you inside out.

So, in truth, I am not wretched.
My friends see in me
Something I can't see in myself-
And I, for that, am very glad.

The best Friend one can have-
Is that of Jesus Christ,
Son of the Living God
Who knows you by heart.

He loves us all so dearly,
He's the sunshine in our lives.
For He knocks at our doors-
Will we love Him in return?

Gratitude

What everyone needs to have
Is a special kind of attitude.
It's not easy to do, but-
This attitude is called gratitude.

Gratitude means to be thankful;
No pouting, whining, or a complaint.
All of us do this at times in our lives,
And if I did it anymore, I'd faint.

I have trouble with gratitude;
I must be taking things for granted.
I try to remember to give thanks,
But I always forget and have ranted.

I watched a movie,
And did learn-
That gratitude is important,
And this is what I yearn.

In the future, I shall try hard, and-
I will remember to have gratitude,
I will not complain or whine;
Mind me that this is a good attitude.

Halftime

Players get here for practice—
He sun is out and shining.
The air is warm to feel,
But a cool breeze blows by.

Practice is underway,
Before the big game starts.
The players run back and forth,
They stretch to avoid hurt.

The game starts a bit late—
Everyone runs to and fro.
It's a tight, hard game,
The other team takes a shot.

Oh! It went into the net!
The whistle blows and—
A foul has been called.
Our team gets the ball.

Back and forth it goes again,
I'm on the edge of my seat.
Yelling and cheering on the teams,
Wish I was out there myself.

Gosh! The other team scores!
It's now one to nothing.
To say I'm a bit peeved
Could be an understatement.

The game plays on,
We keep cheering.
The whistle blows,
And halftime is called.

Isolation

Let me tell you something-
I am in isolation.
I've been in isolation,
I will get out soon.

I will escape this prison.
Contact with the outside world is very little, if any.
We're just confined to our rooms
But we can go outside for air.

This so-called deadly disease
Spreads like wildfire it seems.
People dropping out like flies,
Or like a row of falling dominoes.

Life seems unreal now-
Work, no motivation, food, sleep-
Hard to know what's going on
To stay positive and keep a good outlook.

I'm coming to grips with my sanity-
Oh wait-where'd my sanity go?
The walls are closing in on me…
Or am I just imagining it?

On the bright side it was a good break,
A time for reflection and slowing down.
But I need out of here fast!
I need to see a bit of action!

Life's Mystery

Life is a mystery-
One never knows
What's going to happen
Or what's coming to him.

It all gets so complex-
We can be blinded too.
The world is so noisy
And doesn't help at all.

This virus is a nuisance!
And boy! It ticks me off!
People are going nuts!
And I am going bonkers!

There must be a reason
For what's going on.
I wonder what it is,
When things will get better?

I guess here's a time
For reform and renewal.
"To ponder anew
What the almighty can do."

Goodbye for now, farewell!
Time to focus in life.
Things will get better, I promise-
But when will that be!!??

Mr. Time

Oh where, oh where
Has Mr. Time gone?
He was here one instance
And gone the next!

It seems like yesterday
That I was little.
It seems like yesterday
That I finished high school.

Oh, my dear Mr. Time—
You have been pleasantly missed;
Although for some times
It's not noticed you're amiss.

Please come back Time!
We need you so dearly;
There's not nearly enough of you
To do everything we want to do.

Don't run away from us,
We will not bite.
Some of us may bark,
But rest assured, it's worse than our bite.

Says Mr. Time to myself,
To you and to all:
"My dear good sir,
My dear madame"

"I'm always around—
Here, there, and everywhere!
I'm always here to use,
And I'm here to stay for a while.

Don't be fooled though—
Many a folk thought
That I was endless indeed.
Now those folks have paid for their deeds.

I'm here now,
I'll be here tomorrow.
But will I be here
A month from now?

All things have an end.
All things have a beginning.
Even I, the superb Mr. Time,
Had a beginning and have an end.

I shall not be here forever,
So, budget your time wisely-
Because before you know it
I'll be miles away for good.

Don't wait and procrastinate,
Don't be on a time crunch.
I won't have my good name
Besmirched in this way!

There's a bit of me for this,
And a bit of me for that.
I spread very thin
And stretch far and wide.

Yes, as I said before—
Folks before have paid for their deeds.
They waited too long to change their hearts,
And waited too long to change their ways.

Don't push off till tomorrow
What can be done today.
Don't be the foolish person,
Don't wait to start the game.

It's your choice of course
To take the advice that's mine.
But why wouldn't you want it?
Afterall, I am Mr. Time."

Noise

I'd like to write some poems-
So here I am trying.
We'll see how it goes-
Will it be good or bad?

Working at the bowling alley
With the TV on;
Music ringing out-
Too much for my brain!

How can one focus-
Write any poems,
Say any prayers,
Or even just relax!?

What can I say?
Not much I suppose.
Better try my best,
And focus on this job.

I will get thru it-
Better stay positive-
Keep good thoughts-
Only about 12 days left.

I've come to the end,
Hope it reads well.
Maybe I'll be inspired,
And write another poem.

People, People Everywhere

People, people everywhere
At the tables all around.
People, people everywhere
All sitting on their chairs.

Fresh laughter here and there,
Fills a cafeteria full.
While all enjoy their food,
One sits to write some poetry.

Looking all around this place,
Observing people's traits.
Many people, different traits-
What a wonder it seems to be.

Two guys at a table,
Maybe even three-
Three girls sit at another table,
Sure, I could tell you more!

But this is all for now.
I write this poem for you-
To tell of this certain room,
That's full of laughter and fun.

Productivity

In this day and age,
Time goes by slow,
And time goes by quick,
But I always wonder if I'm productive.

I get up late in the morning,
Eat breakfast and take it slow.
Sometimes I have to tutor,
Other times it's a blank day.

I go to bed late often,
After watching a comedy.
During the day things happen,
And I do whatever needs doing.

But there are days when-
I feel I've done nothing.
Days when I feel groggy,
And days that felt a waste.

I ask myself these questions:
What could I have done today?
What should I do tomorrow?
Why, oh why, was this an unproductive day?

There's more to life, I know.
More to this drudgery I've created.
I will get out of it now!
And start becoming more productive.

I can get up early for Mass,
Find times to pray at Church,
Get busy cooking more often,
And find ways to meet up with friends.

The Beach

I see the waves
Lapping upon the shore.
The swirling sand,
And the foam upon the waters.

The sun shines brightly;
The water sparkles with glee.
Crabs run into their holes,
Feet pound on the sand.

The birds peck away,
And fish jump out of the ocean.
Fishermen waiting to catch a fish,
Swimmer jumping the waves.

Oh, to hear the joy and laughter,
What mirth is on that beach!
Children playing, having fun,
Adults attempting to gain a tan!

People on their boogie boards
Waiting for their wave.
Birds flying through the air,
And dolphins swimming across the waves.

The day ends with calm;
People go home tired,
Ready to sleep and dream
About the day God has gifted them.

Why?

Why are people
The way they are?
How can they be
So mean, so cruel?

There are those few
Who are nice and kind,
But why, oh why
Can't all be nice?

I guess it goes to show
How diverse we are-
The differences we have-
Some things never change.

Let's all try to get along-
With friend and foe.
Maybe one day,
All this will change.

Foe will become friend-
Cruelty turns to sweetness.
Friendship will be a goal,
And there'll be no strife.

I wonder when-
That day will come?
If ever it does-
We just need patience.

Short Verses

A Riddle

What's sweeter than honey
And smells like a rose-
Greater than money
And none can compose?

Autumn

Leaves are falling
Colors shining brightly-
Red, yellow, orange;
What a blessed season!

The Beach

The wind blows in my face-
Waves lap on the shore.
Dolphins leap in the air,
And the sun shines brightly evermore.

I Love You

I stare into His eyes-
He stares into mine.
I say to Him "I love You."
He says "I love you too."

School

My mind is so confused-
There's so much to do.
Grades to be brought up
And classes to be passed.

Chapel

The lights are dim,
The room is quiet,
Candles shine brightly,
What a blessing He has given.

Tabernacle

The door is golden,
Engraved with angels and the Cross.
But the gift inside
Is the best treasure of all.

The Lamb

Jesus is the Lamb,
Who was slain for us.
His blood poured out,
For us to be purified.

Mary

Who is brighter than the sun
And lovelier than the moon?
The purest of all women,
And most blest of all creation?

Thunderstorm

The rains pelt against the windows,
The thunder roars ever so loudly,
Lightning streaks across the sky,
And the sun stays hidden for a time.

About the Author

Abigail Fucci was born in England and currently resides in Virginia with her mom and two younger brothers. She graduated from Seton Catholic High School in 2018 and graduated from Franciscan University of Steubenville in Ohio in December 2021 with a bachelor of arts in clinical psychology. She also received her graduate certificate in criminal justice from Liberty University in the fall of 2023 and is currently working on her associate's degree in paralegal studies with an expected graduation date in the fall or winter of 2024. She loves spending time with friends, family, and her nephews and nieces and thanks God for everything. Abigail became interested in writing after her English class during junior year of high school and now enjoys writing poetry and public speaking. She loves fury animals, the color red, making potholders, reading, bowling, and swimming in the summer. She is a huge mystery fan and loves watching murder mysteries with her mom in addition to old sitcoms. Abigail hopes to work as a full-time paralegal at a law firm, in the claims department for an insurance company, or for a closing company once she finishes her current degree. However, her main aspiration is to become a full-time mother. She also loves old country music and country gospel along with anything Christian. Her message to you is that you are loved, you matter, and that you have purpose. Never give up on life.

Milton Keynes UK
Ingram Content Group UK Ltd.
UKHW052359201024
449919UK00016B/170